# Claude
# **DEBUSSY**

## JEUX
*Poème dansé*
(1913)

Study Score
Partitur

PETRUCCI LIBRARY PRESS

# ORCHESTRA

2 Piccolos

2 Flutes

3 Oboes

English Horn

3 Clarinets

Bass Clarinet

3 Bassoons

Sarrusophone

4 Horns

4 Trumpets

3 Trombones

Tuba

Timpani

Percussion
(Triangle, Tambourine, Cymbals, Xylophone)

2 Harps

Celesta

Violins I

Violins II

Viola

Violoncellos

Double Basses

Duration: ca. 20 minutes

First performance
May 15, 1913, Paris
Paris: Ballets russes
Orchestra / Pierre Monteux

ISBN: 978-1-60874-056-7
This score is a slightly modified unabridged reprint of the score
issued in late 1913 by Durand et Cie., plate D. & F. 8958
The score has been scaled to fit the present format.

Printed in the USA
First Printing: January, 2012

# JEUX
*Poème dansé*

Claude Debussy

4

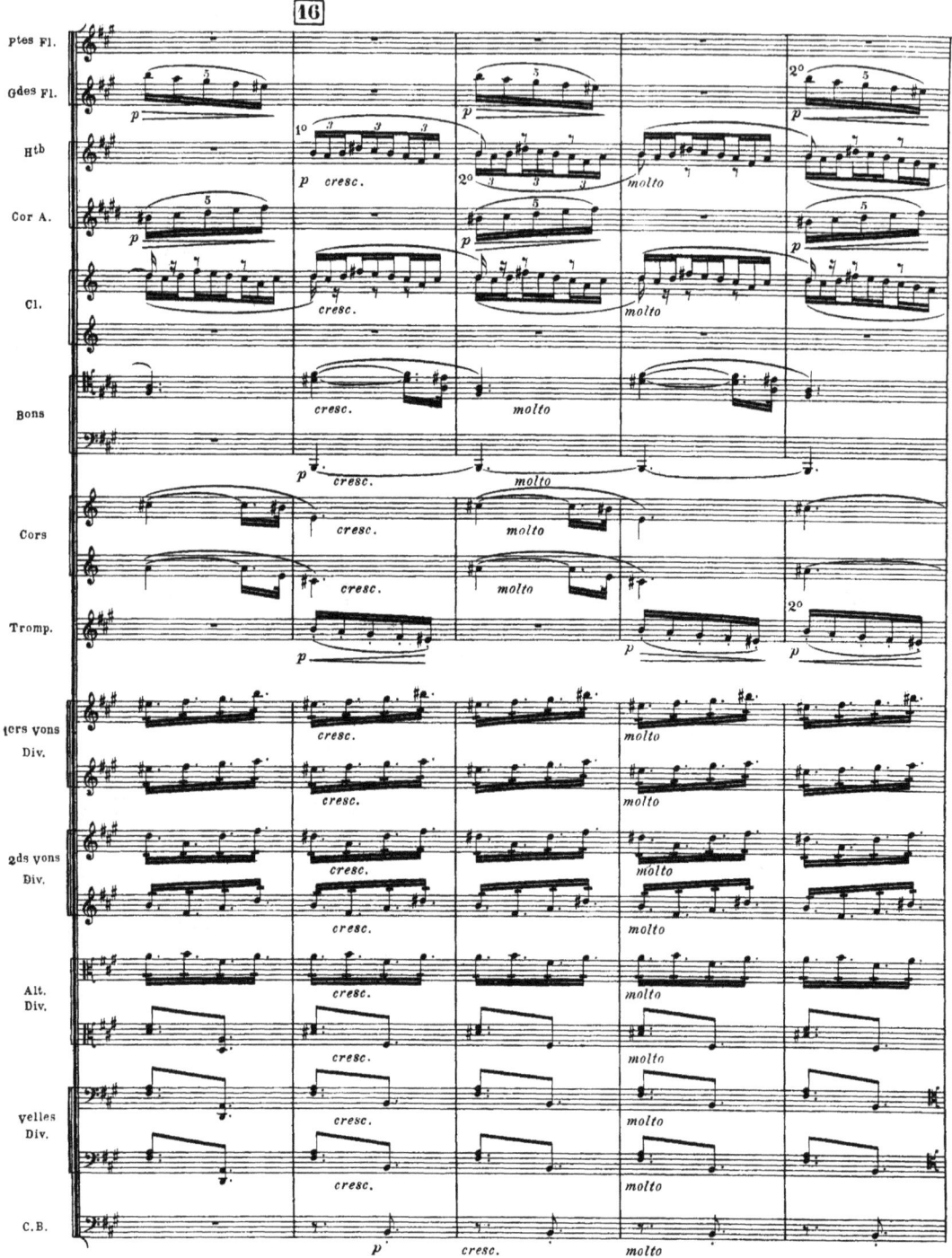

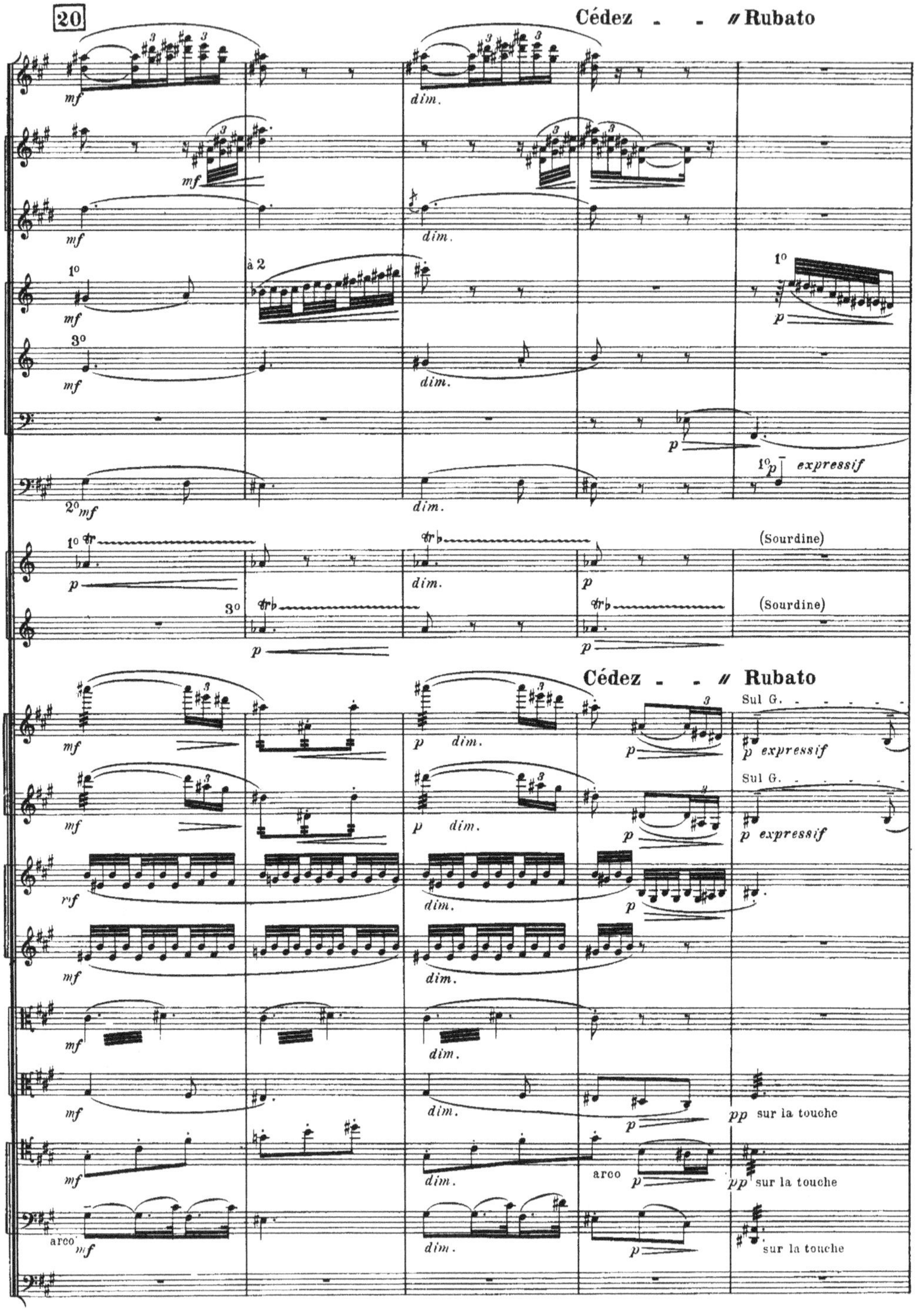
20
Cédez - - // Rubato
Gdes Fl.
Htb
Cor A.
Cl.
Cl. B.
1er et 2e Bons
Cors
(Sourdine)
1ers Vons Div.
2ds Vons Div.
Alt. Div.
Velles Div.
C.B.
expressif
Sul G.
sur la touche
arco

46

57

59

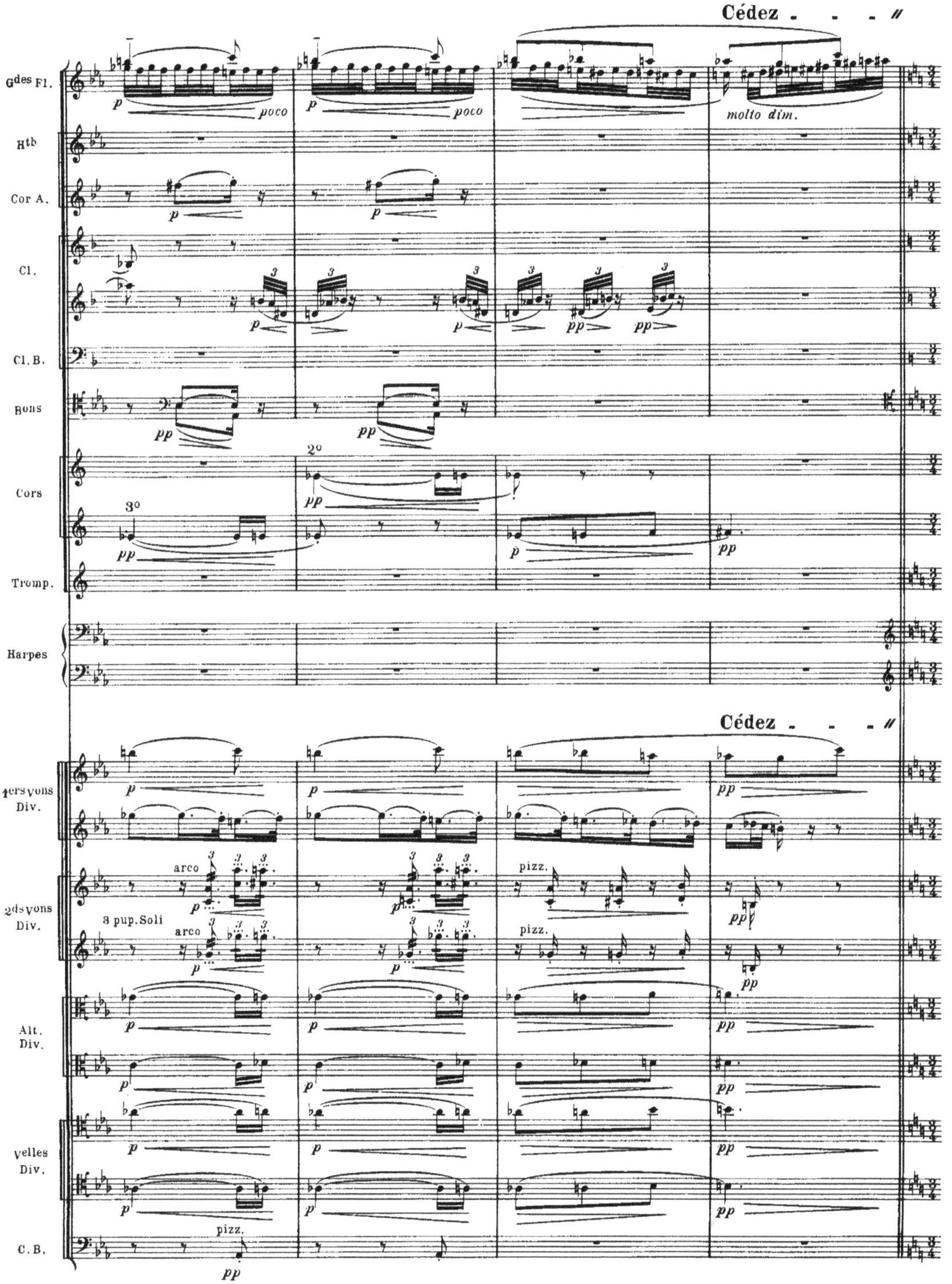
Cédez - - - //
Gdes Fl.
Htb
Cor A.
Cl.
Cl. B.
Bons
Cors
Tromp.
Harpes
p
poco
p
poco
molto dim.
pp
3o
2o
Cédez - - - //
1ers Vons Div.
2ds Vons Div.
3 pup. Soli
arco
pizz.
Alt. Div.
Velles Div.
C. B.
pp

64

79

98

www.ingramcontent.com/pod-product-compliance
Lightning Source LLC
Chambersburg PA
CBHW081347040426
42450CB00015B/3332